Cute Candy Ho

Grayscale Coloring Book for Adults

Fantasy Plasticine Houses, Sweet Fairyland AI Art Designs for Anti Stress & Relaxation

Rachel Mintz

Copyright © 2022 Palm Tree Publishing- All rights reserved.
Images used under license from Shutterstock.com, created with Midjourney AI & Dall-E AI. No part of this publication may be reproduced, distributed, or transmitted in any form or by any means, including photocopying, recording, or other electronic or mechanical methods, without the prior written permission of the publisher, except in the case of brief quotations embodied in critical reviews and certain other noncommercial uses permitted by copyright law.

Scan to join Rachel Mintz printable coloring books club, get coupons, discounts, and free coloring pages.

Visit us on RachelMintz.com

Colors Testing Page

Scan below to order from Amazon

Scan below to order from Amazon

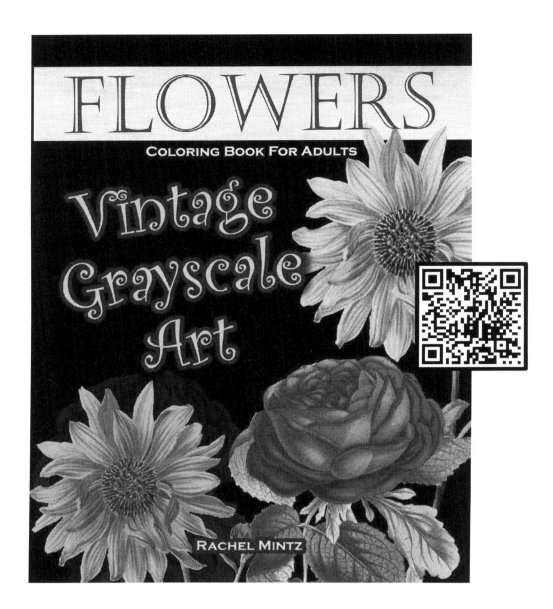

Scan below to order from Amazon

Look for more RACHEL MINTZ coloring books at Amazon.

Mandalas | Wildlife | Marine Life| **Portraits** | Dogs | Cats | **Flowers** | Skulls | Gothic | Architecture | Romantic | Texts & Sayings | Ethnic | Steampunk | **Fashion** | Horses | Unicorns | Witches | Horror | Grayscale | Sports | Christmas | Holidays | Kids | Cars | **Motorbikes** | Trucks | Urban | Fairies | **Jewish Holidays**: Passover, Hanukkah, Purim | Safari | Pets |Multicultural | Educational for Kids | Back to School | **Preschool & Toddlers** | Army & Military | Knights & Castles | Dragons | Princesses | Butterflies | Birds | Reptiles | Bible | **Stained Glass** | Abstract | Machines | **Robots** | Space & Science | **Zombies** | Monsters | And many more topics..

Search Amazon for 'Rachel Mintz coloring books'.

Scan to join Rachel Mintz printable coloring books club, get coupons, discounts, and free coloring pages.

Visit us on RachelMintz.com

Thank you for coloring with us

We will be very thankful if you could take a minute to review THIS book

Printed in Great Britain
by Amazon